Going Back To Retrieve It

Poems by Lorraine Davis

"Meditation on the Sound of Glass Shattering" – *The Awards Anthology,* from the Betty June Siliconas Poetry Center, SCCC, Newton, NJ

"Diving Down Deep" and "Two Poems Hiking" – *Voices from Here,* The Paulinskill Poetry Project

"The Garden" – *The Green Heron Project,* Upper Delaware Writers Collective

"The Blue Serge Sears and Roebuck Man" – *Be Mine Too,* Delaware Valley Arts Alliance

ISBN: 978-0-9824955-9-9

Cover Artwork: Getty Image– *Woman leaving entrance door carrying two suitcases*
Photo credit: Noel Hendrickson
Cover Design: Christopher Reilley

Printed in the United States of America
by Big Table Publishing Company
Boston, MA

BIG TABLE Publishing

bigtablepublishing.com

For all of you who may find yourself the subject of one of these pieces, and for those whose advice and encouragement have meant so much. Special thanks to the members of the Hemlock Farms Writers Group, and my poet friends in New Jersey. A special thanks to Emily N for her editing and to my husband Robert for his technical assistance.

Table of Contents

PART THREE

Part One

"See where the windows are boarded up…
where tiers of oxeye daisies float on a sea of grass?
That's the place to begin."
~ Mark Strand, *Where are the Waters of Childhood*

The Trouble for Poets

The trouble for poets is that so many things
hold the prospect of a poem.

Just last week, driving south
I noticed a faded red wagon
slumbering by the side of a barn.

Instantly it unwrapped a memory of
my favorite photograph
and the design of a poem.

As we crossed over the Delaware
the water below thundered and roared.
The river was high, threatening to
overflow its banks like a defiant child.

Somehow, it brought to mind
the wisdom of an old Buddhist monk
who once counseled:
"If your cup is full, stop pouring."

Later, heading back past rolling hills and
fertile farmland, I glimpsed a well-worn rake
leaning slant against the side of an old wooden shed.

It spoke to me of autumn and a gathering:
pumpkins and squash, corn and beans
and other less tangible things:
recollections, a few regrets
still ripe for harvest.

Back home, I uncover and frame that photograph
of my little daughter pulling her smaller brother
in a well worn red wagon out at the farm.
I place it on my desk.
It's perfect.

I make a note to read more
about Buddhist philosophy.

But the rake outside the shed is insistent.
Like me, it is old and worn
from years of collecting
and storing up
it has stories to tell.

I go back to retrieve it.

Back Then

"In the end of all our exploring
we will arrive where we first started
and know the place
for the first time."
~ T.S. Eliot

The house was solid, substantial
built with oak and brick
grounded, secure.

Each morning the furnace
would come alive, rumbling.

Dad's muted footsteps tread across
the polished hardwood floors.
Then the Buick's engine
coughed to a start
and he was gone.

By noon, the kitchen was humming.
Mama and Grandma stirring up
the evening meal, all the while
murmuring mother-daughter
chatter and sputter.

Grandma rolling out the dough
for her homemade noodles
and famous cinnamon bread.
Mama peeling onions and carrots
for the stew.

In the summer, we picked wild
strawberries in the fields out back
and the large plump ones
from Dad's garden patch.

In the fall, Mama and Grandma
canned up relish and summer fruit
recalling Depression's hunger

I learned soon enough the
secret cranny under the attic rafters
where the Christmas gifts lay hidden.
And later how to remove the screen
from my upstairs bedroom window,
climb out on the roof
and smoke Salems undetected.

I often wonder at the careless ease
of life back then.
The war was over.
Ike was President.
Elvis was King.
We rocked and rolled
through our days
so innocently.
The day after tomorrow
was a long way off
back then.

The Natural

~ for Dad

They say you were a natural.
Quick feet
sure hands
a champion before
talent at sport
got you anything
but the thrill of
playing the game.

Until one Friday night

in a game against
a serious rival
you intercepted a pass
and ran ninety yards
to score the winning touchdown.

From that day on
you were a target.
On the opponents' field
you must have felt like a GI
setting down his boots
on someone else's sacred ground.

Finally

on one bitter Friday night
a burly, gritty tackle
took you down.
You told me you heard a pop

felt the pain shoot
from knee to shin.
It felt like fire.

It was then
on that harsh and hostile field
staggered by pain
that a piece of wisdom came to you:

Being the best
is a coin with two sides-
the curse of the vengeful
the cheers of the crowd.

The Hill

It happened every year
with the first fall of snow.

Pulling on our coats and boots,
we brushed off our sleds and skis
and headed for the hill,

following the familiar path
around the swamp
where we sometimes skated
swirling around the stumps and fallen limbs,

then up the slope
to the crest of the hill
lugging our gear alongside.

It wasn't a sheer or monumental peak,
but in the flat Midwest
it was the best we had.

The first sleds down plowed through
the thick and ungroomed snow
lurching slowly,
composing a fresh and priceless path.

By midday the hill
was swept and slick.
Our Flexible Flyers careened
at breakneck speed.
At the bottom, we hauled them back on foot.
No towropes or lifts on our makeshift hill.

Sometimes, a few of the boys
started a bonfire
to keep us warm, keep us going.

Today I'm sitting at the top of the hill,
a place I come back to often,
to remember myself back
to those worry less days

when future plans were spare,
completely shortsighted:
warm clothes, a hot meal
and plans for the next time
we could go back to
swooshing down the hill.

Early Morning at the Green Parrot Tavern

I walked past it every morning
on my way to school.
The doors were always open
pouring the odor of
beer and smoke
onto the sidewalk.

I always picked up my pace
as I walked by
unnerved by the odor,
the jumble of voices
spilling out into the street,
the dark forbidden nature
of the place.

Much later, I learned
that The Green Parrot was not
the dark and dangerous place
my childhood version
imagined it to be.

It was merely the watering hole
of the night shifters:
Blue collared fathers and brothers who worked
like Dad, on the lines at the plant,
building Oldsmobiles, Buicks and Cadillacs
that they dreamed of owning some day.

Morning was their evening.
Over a beer or two, they eased
their way into noon-night
and woke at sundown to man
the lines again.

The Blue Serge Sears and Roebuck Man

It was before Woodstock
and tie dyes
before Berkeley
and the '68 convention.

On campus, chapel was compulsory
and men wore suits and ties to dinner.

You wore blue serge from Sears and Roebuck
and a tie picturing a moose galumphing
through the mountains
(yes, I did notice.)

One evening, as we were waiting to be served
you asked me out.

So preppy, so serious
I thought to myself.
Probably boring
(but then there was that tie.)

Over dinner downtown, you told me
of the big plans you had for yourself
a PhD in engineering you thought.
Then you forgot to pay the bill.

I forgave you.
I've forgiven you again
        And again
You looked so good in blue back then
You still do.

Flying Lessons

You were our firstborn
confounding from the start.
You fell asleep during feedings
then back in the nursery
you cried because you were hungry
and all alone.

At home, you loved to play undisturbed
spending hours examining the pots and pans
stacking brightly colored blocks just so.

We tiptoed through the house
not wanting to interfere with your design.
Sometimes you fell asleep
draped over the blocks
exhausted by such deep and earnest labor.

Nighttimes were more perplexing.
Tucked tightly in your crib
we tried to sleep
anguished by your cries.
We had abandoned you
you seemed to think,.
never to return again.

By four or five you'd found your wings
learned to roller skate
flirt with the boys at school
sing, take dancing lessons
Oh, how you loved to dance.

But sometimes the rowdy and bullish
insolence of the schoolyard
unsettled you
sent you winging back home
like a small fledgling bird
returning to its nest
a softer, safer place
to dance and play.

But you knew, even then
that you couldn't stay there forever.
Your flying lessons had begun.

Hitting the Sweet Spot

Ever hit a baseball on the sweet spot?
You can feel it, hear it.
There's nothing like it
nothing sweeter.

Remember, son, when you
got into one of those "zones?"
Everything you swung at
made that sound
as the ball sailed
looking like it might
stay airborne forever.

Finally, the streak ended
like they always do.
Even A-Rod has slumps.
Life is not sweet endlessly.

But you keep swinging,
chasing the feel of it
the sound of it
because there's nothing like it
nothing sweeter.

Reunion

~ For D.P. on the occasion of our
  50th high school reunion

You walked me home from school every day
then jogged back to your place
on the other side of town.

But I brushed you off, over and over
because you were a geek, long before geekiness ruled.

I've thought often of you through the years
as if some unnamed force drew me
to that memory from long ago.

Then, all these years later, we'd meet again.
You'd ride your Harley from your home
in the high plains of Colorado
to the Great Lakes
and the little town
where we grew up
for our final class
reunion.

Turns out you'd joined the Air Force
out of high school,
become a computer geek,
married an archeologist from Nova Scotia,
had a son,
got divorced,
then married her again.

Grey mustached, tougher and wiser
than you were back then,
there was a quiet gentleness about you
as if you'd made your peace with the world.

So glad we got to meet
for one last time.

Part Two

When God demanded light
He didn't banish darkness.
Instead He invented
ebony and crows
and the small mole
on your left cheekbone.

~ Linda Pastan, *Why Are Your Poems So Dark?*

Meditation on the Sound of Glass Shattering

I can recall
a time or two
hearing the sound
of glass shattering.

Once, when our son
in a teen-age pique
put his fist
through a plate glass window

another when my car
made an intimate acquaintance
with a tree
on a winding road
near Promised Land State Park

That sound never implies promise
that I know of.

Instead, even after the pieces
have been swept away
the rubble removed
the wounds healed

the tiniest of shards remain.
easy to step on
and open a wound
as you're brushing off
the counter, or something else.

They take up residence
just under the skin
sometimes forever,
piercing reminders
of the sound of glass shattering.

The Good Neighbor

~ For Mrs. M

You were our anchor.
While others came then left
you were steadfast.

Each spring we'd watch you
plant new begonias.
Don't put them out too early.
You'd always say.
Before mid-month
There's still a chance for frost.

In the summer you'd water and weed.
Your peonies would bloom.
We'd watch the blue spruce you planted as a seedling
grow tall and proud and flourish.

In the evenings you'd sit outside.
Sometimes we'd sit down with you
and linger as you recalled
how your Fred sneezed and lost his dentures
while cultivating the garden.
(You never did find them)
Or how your Uncle August hid his money
in a bud vase
(enough to pay for his funeral)

On gloomy days the phone would sometimes ring.
"It's going to storm,"
You'd always say.
"I'm feeling stiff."

So we'd gather our boots and umbrellas
and come for tea.

Yesterday, a friend came to gather your flowers
in remembrance.
Today, the neighbor's cat curls up on your doorstep.
It seems perplexed.
We come and go as if everything is the same.
But nothing will ever be
exactly the same again.

Diagnosis

~ For my friend, Susie P.

It came like a bolt on a perfectly cloudless day.
And before we could breathe in its essence
you were gone.
We'll never breathe quite so carelessly again.

Diving Down Deep

We've always liked
living
close to the water.

I'm drawn to it.
Soothed by the lap of the waves
coming ashore.
Spellbound by its blue-green surface
Buoyed by the feel of it
on my skin
in the heat of the summer.

But you, my love,
insist on diving deep down.
Donning goggles and gear
you slip beneath the surface
searching for whatever
lies beneath.

Once
in a cold Canadian lake
you dove down deep.

I watched from the shore.
searching
for a sign
that you had resurfaced.

I saw none.

My heart turned cold.
I pictured you
f l o a t i n g

washing up on some
far-off distant shore.

"He's not coming up!"
I screamed.

And then you did.

Isn't it the way
we've always been?

You, diving down deep
Me, waiting
anxious and fretful
on the shore.

On the Photograph of our Son Holding his Infant Daughter
~ Remembering kjd

He sits quietly
cradling her tiny head
in his strong and weathered hands.

All dreams stolen by her breathlessness
seized by some inscrutable unforeseen.
So beautiful, so whole
Stillborn

Still born.

Night Sky in November

moon rising early
stark stripped trees
their nakedness exposed
like a grief undiluted.

The Last Aunt

"She is like a horse grazing
  a hill pasture that someone makes
  smaller by coming every night
  to pull the fences in and in."
~ Jane Kenyon, *In the Nursing Home*

She's in a "home" now.
On good days she plays cards
with the others.
On bad days we wonder
where she is.

Perhaps a small child again
watching Uncle Bill pull up
in his Durant touring car
the back loaded with groceries.
Times were hard back then.

Or posing for pictures
on her wedding day
dressed in her best dress
and a flowered hat.

The nurse comes in.
"Time for your evening pills"
she says.

Aunt does not complain.
The spaces of her life, smaller now:
This room, her bed, her desk, her chair
herself waiting…waiting….

Our Daughter's Hair

Even those who met you only once
remembered you for your long golden hair.
Once, years ago, your little kittens, climbed up those strands
and made a nest in it.

It came off in patches
grew whispy, unruly.
Finally you shaved it
mourning its loss
hating what chemo has done.

Boomerang

How often do we think some painful memory from long ago
has been thoroughly and completely dismissed, buried
only to find that it has just been taking
a long and peaceful nap?

The awakening of those memories brings to mind
an incident from another time another place.
a memory about memories, so to speak.

It was a day in early spring
cloudless, magnificent.
The children were out in the yard
trying their skill with something new,
a boomerang.

Throwing it as far as they could out into the yard,
it doubled back, just like it's supposed to do
whistling through the shattered space in the window of the garage
where an errant baseball had gone
some days before.

What were the odds of such a trajectory?
It was as if it held within itself the memory of that broken space
doubling back to break open an old wound
still unrepaired.

Finding Some Balance

Remember the seesaws we played on
when we were young?

Some of my schoolmates played
with one on each end,
but I preferred a different game.

Walking up one end
until I reached the center,
I would shift my weight carefully
until both ends balanced perfectly mid-air.

Today
I imagine myself back on that old seesaw
struggling to maintain balance,
wondering if it is my ageing body
that is making it so hard.

or if the ground itself has
become unsteady,
shifting and searching for a
firm and unwavering
center to
stand
on.

Part Three

So be sure when you step
step with care and great tact.
And remember that life's
a great balancing act.
~ Dr. Seuss, *Oh the Places You'll Go*

Vocabulary

Browsing through my pile of poems,
I notice that particular words show up
again, and again
like the stray cat we thought we had
convinced to go away.

Words like *fretful, and unforeseen;*
Phrases like *glass shattering, dreams broken*

Should I take a vow to expand my lexicon?
Find the stray cat a forever home?
embrace more uplifting words like *serenity,*
soul-stirring, saunter, and serendipity
 rhododendron, potpourri, aphrodisiac.

I want to celebrate the small pleasures

catching the brilliant red of a cardinal
as it streaks past the window
a dash of color against the slate grey
of late February

waking to the aroma of fresh coffee
sweet and bold
urging me to throw off my warm covers

watching our cat cuddled
in his favorite sun spot
just under the window

even on the darkest days,
the gift of some small pleasure

On the Photograph of Grandpa and Me

It must have been a Sunday
in late fall.
He's wearing his good suit
and top hat.

I am an exuberant three,
decked out fashionably
in a wool overcoat
and matching bonnet.

I have him by the hand
leading him
showing the way.

I must have been too young, untamed
to have learned my lessons well:
Not to lead, but to follow
To speak little, listen well.

Today, ripened, weathered
unruly, impolite,
I'm threading my way towards
three again.

Two Poems Hiking

This one's wearing bulky wafflestompers
and tramps heavily
leaving a crush of sweet violets
under its bootstep.

This one, in dainty sandals,
treads lightly
stopping to pick a small bouquet
and admire the wild geraniums
along the trail.

Finally, at path's end
they meet
to dine on cheese and cabernet
on a cloth spread out
ready for sweet refreshment.

Watching the Cat Sleep

"I wish I could write as mysterious as a cat."
~ Edgar Allen Poe

In his sleep, he paws the air.
I'm thinking maybe he's fallen into the neighbor's swimming pool
and is kitty-paddling frantically to reach the ladder,
or racing toward some reckless rendezvous with an unknown
female feline.

Finally, the pawing stops.

He must be lying by the warmth of the fire.
wearing his favorite pajamas.

The Garden

Mother loved her pansies.
Multicolored, faces up, smiling,
they encircled the tall and stately
daffodils and tulips.

Around the corner,
Dad's French lilac flowered,
dusky hued,
spreading its delicate fragrance
overflowing.

As for me, I loved the vinca,
a creeper set obscurely
on a shady bank out back,
spreading a green and glossy blanket,
tendrils gripping to gain footing
in the tough and merciless clay.

In summer, tiny blue blossoms
sprouted among the vines.
Small children loved to pick bouquets of them,
wading through the tangled mass to reach them.

If I had one wish,
it would be to grow like that vinca,
not showy, but tenacious, persistent
forever seeking out new spaces to expand and grow,
and every summer offering petite bouquets
of sweet blue flowers to little children.

The Big Brick House of my Childhood

Let it go, let it go.

Just driving by, I notice the wren house in the backyard is vacant
and hollow
where once we greeted those chatty little nomads
who flocked and flourished.

Let it go, let it go

The new owners have put on neon blue shutters
and an awkward addition.

Let it go, let it go

I breathe in the scent of the French lilac
Dad planted years ago
flowering with loss.

Let it go, let it go.

Let these owners fashion their own memories
in the big brick house of my childhood

Let it go, let it go, let it go.

About the Author

A Michigan native, Lorraine received her BA in English Literature from Alma College and did additional work at Michigan State and Central Michigan University while pursuing a teaching career. Always interested in writing, she has worked more seriously since joining several poetry and writing groups. She has had work published in *The Journal of Poetry Therapy* and several anthologies and journals in New York, New Jersey and Pennsylvania. She and her husband Robert live in Hemlock Farms along with their three seriously pampered cats.

A Message from Lorraine Davis

Dear Reader,

I hope that reading this book has been a good experience for you. If it has, I expect that you can think of other people who would appreciate it. Here's how you could help them and me. Many books are competing for readers' attention, and the most important way for a book to get more notice is for readers to write favorable reviews and post them on Amazon.com.

The more positive reviews or comments a book gets, the more it moves up the ranking for exposure when people search on Amazon. When a book has ten reviews it becomes eligible to be included in the "also bought" and "you might like" recommendations. These listings add to the number of books likely to be purchased and read.

But if you don't want to write a review, please take a few minutes to read and rate reviews posted by other readers. Just the act of "liking" a review moves it up the queue in which they appear.

Thanks in advance for your effort to boost the distribution and exposure of this book.